France

Tradition, Culture, and Daily Life

MAJOR NATIONS IN A GLOBAL WORLD

Books in the Series

Australia

Brazil

China

France

Germany

India

Italy

Japan

Mexico

Russia

South Africa

United Kingdom

France

Tradition, Culture, and Daily Life

MAJOR NATIONS IN A GLOBAL WORLD

Richard Garratt

Mason Crest

Mason Crest
450 Parkway Drive, Suite D
Broomall, PA 19008
www.masoncrest.com

Printed and bound in the United States of America.

First printing
9 8 7 6 5 4 3 2 1

Series ISBN: 978-1-4222-3339-9
ISBN: 978-1-4222-3343-6
ebook ISBN: 978-1-4222-8583-1

The Library of Congress has cataloged the hardcopy format(s) as follows:

Library of Congress Cataloging-in-Publication Data

Garratt, Richard.
  France / by Richard Garratt.
     pages cm. -- (Major nations in a global world: tradition, culture, and daily life)
  Includes index.
  ISBN 978-1-4222-3343-6 (hardback) -- ISBN 978-1-4222-3339-9 (series) -- ISBN 978-1-4222-8583-1 (ebook)
  1. France--Juvenile literature. 2. France--Social life and customs--Juvenile literature. I. Title.
  DC17.G37 2015
  944--dc23
                              2015005025

Developed and produced by MTM Publishing, Inc.
        Project Director   Valerie Tomaselli
        Copyeditor   Lee Motteler/Geomap Corp.
        Editorial Coordinator   Andrea St. Aubin

Indexing Services   Andrea Baron, Shearwater Indexing

Art direction and design by Sherry Williams, Oxygen Design Group

Contents

Introduction. 6

1 History, Religion, and Tradition 9

2 Family and Friends. 17

3 Food and Drink 25

4 School, Work, and Industry 33

5 Arts and Entertainment 41

6 Cities, Towns, and the Countryside 49

Further Research. 56

Series Glossary. 57

Index 59

Photo Credits 63

About the Author. 64

KEY ICONS TO LOOK FOR:

Words to Understand: These words with their easy-to-understand definitions will increase the reader's understanding of the text, while building vocabulary skills.

Sidebars: This boxed material within the main text allows readers to build knowledge, gain insights, explore possibilities, and broaden their perspectives by weaving together additional information to provide realistic and holistic perspectives.

Research Projects: Readers are pointed toward areas of further inquiry connected to each chapter. Suggestions are provided for projects that encourage deeper research and analysis.

Text-Dependent Questions: These questions send the reader back to the text for more careful attention to the evidence presented there.

Series Glossary of Key Terms: This back-of-the book glossary contains terminology used throughout this series. Words found here increase the reader's ability to read and comprehend higher-level books and articles in this field.

The Louvre Museum in Paris.

INTRODUCTION

France is a country of vibrant culture and traditions, all part of a complex past at the heart of European, even world, history. Its legendary cathedrals in the centers of small towns and cities; its chateaus, or castles, dotting the countryside; and its manor houses are all remnants of the past that still shape its present.

While steeped in tradition, France has embraced the new and modern, beginning with one of the world's symbols of modernity—the Eiffel Tower. The country has produced pioneering innovation and invention, world-class exponents of all branches of the arts, and food and drink of the highest standards. With a diverse geography—from high, snowy mountains to flat and fertile plains, from vibrant global cities to quaint rural villages—the French people share a way of life that runs deep with tradition and earns the famous French phrase, *joie de vivre*—a joy of living.

Tour Eiffel in Paris.

WORDS TO UNDERSTAND

annul: to declare an official agreement, decision, or result invalid.

impoverish: to make poor; to exhaust the strength of.

mecca: a place that attracts people with particular interests.

CHAPTER 1

History, Religion, and Tradition

While the historical record tells us that France has been inhabited for tens of thousands of years, the modern nation that we know of as France only really took shape in the late 1700s, when a far-reaching, profound political revolution established the country's modern ideas about liberty and equality.

CAVE PAINTINGS
The first evidence of man in France goes back as far as 40,000 BCE. Indeed, there are examples of prehistoric cave paintings dating to 30,000 BCE found in Lascaux.

Evidence of Roman rule—amphitheaters, aqueducts, temples—can be seen across France. Pictured here is the Pont du Gard, a Roman aqueduct built over the Gard River in the southeast.

Originally called Gaul, the country of France was populated by Celts who arrived from the east to settle with the farmers already working the land. In 51 BCE, Julius Caesar conquered Gaul and the area was gradually integrated into the Roman Empire.

Towards the end of the fifth century, Gaul was overrun by the Germanic Francs who dominated the region for hundreds of years. In 911, the Normans (Norsemen) from Scandinavia then began to rule, and in 1066, the Duke of Normandy, or William the Conqueror, invaded England, and for over 400 years French became the language of the upper classes of England.

During the Middle Ages, roughly from the 900s through the 1400s, the Capetian Dynasty ruled in France, though it struggled to control independent rulers in across the country. During this time, the feudal system developed in France, through which vassals pledged loyalty to their lords and serfs worked the land. A key development in this period was the marriage of the Capetian king Louis VII to Eleanor of Aquitaine, which gave him considerable power. Their marriage failed, however, and was eventually **annulled** by the Pope. Eleanor married again in 1154, this time to the young English king, Henry II of the House of Plantagenet.

After 1328 with the death of Charles IV "the Fair," a crisis followed as there was no direct successor, which led to the Hundred Years' War between the House of Valois and the House of Plantagenet, but effectively a war between France and England. The tide turned to the Valois later in the war, and a sense of nationalism was awakened when a young peasant girl, Joan of Arc, led the

French forces to victory, ultimately forcing the English out of France.

The victory gave the French kings considerable power, and a centralized absolute monarchy developed. Over the next three centuries, France, having invaded Italy and seeing its cultural riches, experienced the Renaissance. The country blossomed both economically and culturally.

Protestantism spread under François I, but conflict between the Huguenots (the Protestants) and Catholics, accustomed to dominance in the region, steadily grew under his son Henry II. The French Wars of Religion (1562–1598) resulted, during which between 2 and 4 million people were killed. After becoming king, Henry IV, a Huguenot, converted to Catholicism to bring peace to the country and issued the Edict of Nantes, which gave certain rights to the Huguenots, thus ending the conflict.

ST. BARTHOLOMEW'S DAY MASSACRE

During the Wars of Religion, Henry II's wife, Catherine de Medici, ordered the killing of thousands of Protestants in the St. Bartholomew's Day Massacre in 1572.

A painting, *Saint Bartholomew's Day Massacre*, by François Dubois, a Huguenot artist. To the left in the background, Catherine de Medici is shown emerging from the Château du Louvre to inspect a heap of bodies.

In 1682, Louis XIV relocated his court to Versailles, not far from Paris. It was so admired that other European kingdoms tried to copy its design.

In 1643 Louis XIV came to the throne. Known as the Sun King, he believed in the "divine right of kings," claiming that the only being above a king was God. During his autocratic reign, war with France's European rivals was almost constant. By the end of his rule, France was nearly **impoverished**.

The excesses under Louis XIV fuelled discontent, which led to a major turning point in the country's history. In 1789 the French Revolution overthrew the monarchy and the country was governed as a republic. The motto "Liberté, égalité, fraternité" (freedom, equality, fraternity) was coined and has shaped the country's approach to democracy ever since. Between the start of the Revolution and 1794, some 20,000 people had been executed. Executions were considered a diversion with people jostling for the best places to watch. It is no wonder this period was known as the Reign of Terror.

France's rival powers—Austria, Britain, Naples, the Netherlands, Prussia, and Spain—would try to contain its growing ambitions in Europe. However, their forces suffered a defeat at Toulon by the revolutionary army that increased the renown of Napoleon Bonaparte, one of the most famed rulers in world history. Napoleon I became emperor of France in 1804, establishing the First French Empire.

Napoleon created a constitution with a system of laws aimed at eliminating discrimination and corruption. He also promoted education in the arts and science and, following a meeting with the Pope, restored respect for religion.

Through his military genius, Belgium, the Netherlands, Germany, Austria, the Italian states, and Spain were added to France's empire. To secure his power, Napoleon installed his brother, Joseph Bonaparte, as king of Spain, as well of Naples and Sicily in today's southern Italy.

But it was his campaign against Russia that was his undoing. Suffering from exhaustion and the severe winter, Napoleon and his army retreated from Russia in late 1812, and other countries successfully fought for the return of their lands. Napoleon abdicated in 1814 and went into exile on the island of Elba. The country reverted to monarchy in 1814 when Louis XVI's younger brother, Louis XVIII, became king. Napoleon I, however, came out of exile and led his army once more, culminating in a final defeat at the Battle of Waterloo in 1815.

During the reign of Charles X, workers grew more and more disillusioned with their lack of rights, and he was deposed in 1830. In May 1848 an armed uprising occurred and by the year's end, Louis Napoleon Bonaparte, nephew of Napoleon I, became France's first elected president. But when he was limited by the constitution from a second term, he seized power and became the emperor of the Second French Empire. Although he promised a peaceful rule, Napoleon III, as

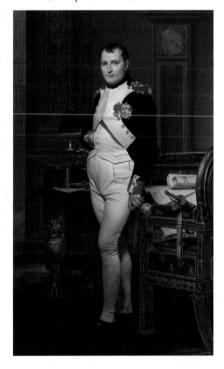

he was known, entered into major wars, including the Crimean War (1854–1856), followed almost immediately by the Second Opium War against China. The Franco-Prussian War (1870–1871) ended with Napoleon III surrendering to German troops.

Following this defeat and the tough conditions imposed by the Germans, a new government was set up, beginning the Third Republic. As the nineteenth century drew to a close, the country at last saw prosperity and peace. Interest in the arts grew with movements such as Impressionism and Art Nouveau. In 1889 the Exposition Universelle sponsored the building of the Eiffel Tower, a "temporary" structure that lasts to this day, becoming one of France's best-known landmarks.

The Emperor Napoleon in His Study at the Tuileries (1812), by Jacques-Louis David.

Peace was not to last, however, as decades, indeed centuries, of mistrust among European powers led again to war. France was taken by surprise at the outbreak of World War I (1914–1918). The loss of life was staggering by the time France and its allies, including Britain and eventually the United States, finally won the war.

Reconstruction of the country began in earnest in the all-too-short period before 1940, one year into World War II. By June of that year, France had surrendered to Nazi Germany, which occupied just under half of the country with a pro-Nazi "puppet" government based in Vichy, central France. The Allied Forces of the United States, Britain, and Canada invaded on D-Day, June 6, 1944, and Paris was liberated on August 25th of that year.

General Charles de Gaulle served briefly as president right after the war and regained the presidency in 1958, serving until 1969. In May 1968, unrest among students—unhappy with capitalism—quickly spread to factories, where masses of workers went on strike for two weeks. De Gaulle called for new parliamentary elections, and the violence came to an end.

REGIONAL DIVERSITY AND CHEESE!

 President Charles de Gaulle famously said, in celebrating the regional diversity of France and its people, "How can you govern a country that has 246 varieties of cheese!"

Since the 1970s, leaders from both the right and left have been in power. While problems plague the country—such as the unrest of immigrants from its former African colonies and high rates of unemployment—it remains one of the world's major industrial powers and a vibrant cultural **mecca**. Its turbulent history has surely enriched *le patrimoine*—its heritage.

U.S. troops landing in the Normandy invasion on D-Day in June 1944.

TEXT-DEPENDENT QUESTIONS

1. Describe the feudal system in France in the Middle Ages.

2. What were the outcomes of the two twentieth-century world wars in France?

RESEARCH PROJECTS

1. Create a timeline of Napoleon I's life and achievements, along with a short summary of his role in French history.

2. Examine the picture of the Pont du Gard in this chapter and research its design. Write a brief report about the design, especially the use of arches across its span, and how Roman architects employed it in other structures.

General Charles De Gaulle leading a parade celebrating the liberation of Paris on August 26, 1944.

Family and friends at the promenade of the old port in Marseille.

WORDS TO UNDERSTAND

fortnight: a period of fourteen days.

insular: closed in and insulated from outside ideas and people.

CHAPTER 2

Family and Friends

The family has been a central part of French society throughout its history, and its influence is still widely felt. It is the social adhesive of the country, and every family member has responsibilities and duties.

French families used to be large. It wasn't uncommon for a couple to have over ten children. Nowadays the norm is two. There were also more marriages in the past, but the number has decreased since the end of the1960s. The number fell by 25 percent in the 1970s and 1980s, while the number of couples living together—including same-sex couples—has greatly increased. Since 1999, couples of the same sex often enter into a Civil Solidarity Pact (com-

Young mother and daughter having breakfast together in a Parisian café.

monly known as PACS) as this gives the couple legal rights, although not as many as through marriage. French law dictates that a couple must get married in the local town hall before any other ceremony.

THE STATE AND THE FAMILY

In order to obtain benefits allowed families, people must deal with French administration and bureaucracy, which can be monumental. Sometimes it takes a very long time to get things done; nevertheless, the level of support is considerable.

The family is highly valued in France and the government's support structures reflect that. The mother of a baby has the right to sixteen weeks of 100 percent-paid maternity leave. If there is already another child in the family, this can be extended to twenty-six weeks, and if the mother is expecting twins, the maternity leave can go up to thirty-four weeks. The father also has the right to three days leave at the time of the birth followed by eleven days of paid leave to be taken within the first four months after the birth. A further six months leave can be taken by either of the parents (if they are both employed) following the end of the maternity leave.

The State actively encourages the creation of families. After the birth of a second child, the family receives a monthly allowance. A third child more than doubles the monthly allowance, with subsequent children upping it even more.

The French class system, which categorizes individuals and families according to social status and ownership of property, is less pronounced than in the days of the monarchy. It still affects, however, how certain people interact with each other. For instance, the *haute bourgeoisie* ("high bourgeois"), which is the highest class, fiercely guard themselves against the *nouveau riche* ("new money"), which refers to people who hope to raise their social status simply because they have become rich.

TOP CLASS

France's *haute bourgeoisie* is a social rank that includes families dating back to the French Revolution. They are sometimes referred to as the 200 families, a name given at the beginning of the twentieth century.

The expression "France Profonde," a slightly derogatory term, refers to another group of people in France, mainly rural-living folk, almost peasants. They live simply and are **insular** in their outlook. In fact, they seldom travel far from their villages, even to go to the main city of their *department* (large administrative area). A trip to the French capital, Paris, or one of the other major cities, such Bordeaux in the west or Marseilles in the south, is a very rare adventure.

The French like getting together and having parties, and this includes families! The extended family often meets for such events as baptisms or birthdays, but they also get together for quite simple reasons. It is not unusual, for example, to see large groups of family members gathered round an outside table podding *haricot sec*, a type of bean—available for a very short period in the year and usually sold in huge sacks. A glass of wine makes the conversation flow and the job is done quickly!

A mansion in the baroque style of architecture common in Paris and its environs during the seventeenth and eighteenth centuries.

Time off is important to French families and annual vacation time is very generous. Five weeks paid holiday is the legal number, but there is also a system of rewarding employees who work more than the maximum thirty-five hours a week. This is called RTT—*Réduction du Temps de Travail* (Reduction of Working Time) and can amount to a further twenty-two days. And on top of that there are eleven days of "bank holidays." So nine and a half weeks of time off annually is not unusual.

During the annual summer vacations of August, and sometimes July, families take to the roads *en masse* and go to the coast or mountains. This is when the family really spends time together. Sometimes grandparents go along with them. Some inland towns can seem quite empty during the month, with shops and even restaurants closed on their *congé annuel*.

TIME OFF

In 1936, following a general strike, an agreement was signed that guaranteed, among other rights, a two-week paid vacation for every worker. This gave factories and other businesses the opportunity to shut down for a **fortnight** so that every worker would go on vacation at the same time. It also led to the generous vacation periods the French workers currently enjoy.

Enjoying the sun and water at Nice, on the French Riviera, during the annual summer holiday.

A kiss on both cheeks is the traditional way of greeting friends and saying goodbye.

When a couple meets with a group of friends, the woman will greet everyone with a kiss on each cheek, while the man will shake hands with his male friends and kiss the females on both cheeks. In some regions it is four kisses. This is known as "*faire la bise*," literally "to make the kiss." If two males know each other particularly well they may also kiss each other on both cheeks as well. You can imagine that in large groups of friends it can take some time to say hello!

This tradition has been in place for some time and is all part of French etiquette. Another demonstration of these standards of politeness is when one encounters a stranger. For instance, when entering a shop or meeting someone in the street, people show their respect with the greetings "Bonjour, monsieur" or "Bonjour, madame," meaning "Good day, sir" or "Good day, madame."

Some say that it is hard to make true friends in France. Most long-term friendships are made at school, although work, education, and hobbies do give the opportunity to make friends. However, with family life so important, at the end of a workday many people will get home as quickly as possible to enjoy time together. A quick drink in a bar after work is common, but long-term and deep friendships with work colleagues are not typical.

When invited to a meal or an event at a friend's house, a gift is expected, such as flowers, chocolates, a bottle of wine—and sometimes all three! For "family day," when the meal is usually at lunchtime (Sunday is very often the day for this), the meal can last a long time. It will include aperitifs with their accompanying nibbles, followed by the meal itself, and then coffee. The guests may arrive at around 12:30 and can still be at the table at 5 o'clock in the afternoon!

GETTING TOGETHER WITH FAMILY

Evening meals are usually taken *en famille* and are very important, for it is then that everybody discusses their day, including its highs and lows. Also, most people tend to live in the region where they grew up and so weekend visits to see parents or grandparents are common.

Family and friends are very important to the people of France, but everyone needs to know their place. For example, it is easy in English to say "you" when you are speaking to someone, but in French there are two ways of saying it: *vous* for everyone but your close friends and *tu* for only close friends and members of your family. Even the latter requires the respect of age, for young people have to be invited to *tu-toi* members of the older generation. And degrees of friendship are explained in different ways. Paradoxically, if someone was to say "this is my good friend," that person wouldn't be as close as someone described as "this is my friend." If you have to say more about a person, then you may actually be saying less. Complicated, isn't it?!

Respect for the older generation is important in France. Shown here is a parade in honor of Grandmother's Day in Paris in 2011. The signs say "I ♥ my grandmother.

TEXT-DEPENDENT QUESTIONS

1. Name two government regulations that help support families in France.

2. What is the *haute bourgeoisie* in France?

RESEARCH PROJECTS

1. Research French etiquette and develop a list of four to five customs that illustrate the importance the society places on politeness and proper interpersonal interactions. Develop a similar list for the United States or another country you are familiar with.

2. Develop a statistical portrait of the French population by preparing a table of data on changes in the French population from 1950 to 2015. Use at least three types of factors—such as growth rate of population, birth rate, and literacy rate.

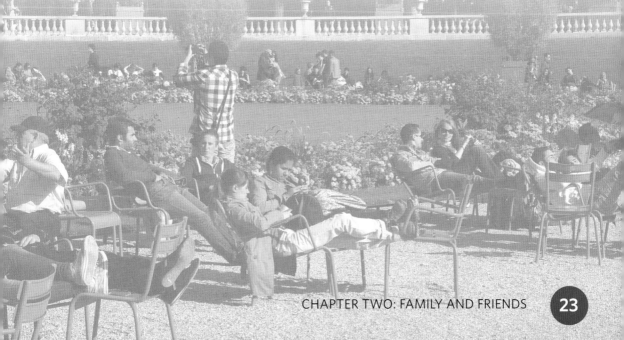

Family and friends enjoy themselves on a sunny day at the Luxembourg Gardens in Paris.

A typical café in the Montmartre district of Paris.

WORDS TO UNDERSTAND

engender: to cause to develop.

fermentation: a chemical change that helps to create the alcoholic content of wine and other beverages.

gastronomic: relating to good cooking and eating.

hotelier: a person running a hotel.

intangible: not physical; unable to be perceived through touch.

CHAPTER 3

Food and Drink

"The French live to eat while everyone else eats to live"—this well-known saying defines the French outlook on one of life's basic pleasures. Eating and its enjoyment shape daily routines, spark much conversation, and even **engender** passion and patriotism.

The tradition of fine cooking goes back centuries in France. Originally it was heavily influenced by Italian cuisine, but in the seventeenth century, movements shifted French cooking away from its foreign origins to its own native style. Today it has a world-class reputation. The "French **gastronomic** meal" was recognized in 2010 by UNESCO as a notable example of "**Intangible** Cultural Heritage."

Tartiflette savoyarde, from the Alps.   Bouillabaisse, the classic fish soup, of Marseille.

The UN organization deemed it a "social custom aimed at celebrating the most important moments in the lives of individuals and groups."

France is the third largest country in Europe (after Russia and Ukraine), and its differing geography, farming, and fishing create regional dishes quite distinct from each other. In the mountains such as the Alps, there are many cheese-based dishes, such as *fondue savoyarde,* cheese melted with white wine and garlic served with chunks of bread; raclette, coming from the word *racler* to scrape, where the cheese is heated until a layer starts to melt, scraped off, and served over boiled potatoes; and *tartiflette,* a baked dish of potatoes, onions, and bacon topped with cheese. In the south, originating from the port of Marseille, bouillabaisse, a fish and shellfish stew, is popular. From the northeast comes andouillette, a coarse-grained sausage encased in pork intestines. Along the river Loire, fish like pike or zander are served with a beurre blanc sauce made from butter, vinegar or white wine, and shallots.

A HAPPY ACCIDENT

The origins of the dessert tarte tatin, an upside-down tart with fruit—usually apples—are intriguing. According to some, a **hotelier** Stéphanie Tatin was cooking an apple pie one day but forgot the apples cooking on the stove. When she smelled burning, she tried to rescue the dish: she put the pastry on the top and the whole pan in the oven. She flipped it over to serve, and—voila!—it became an instant success.

While regional specialities help define local customs, certain dishes have national significance. Some starters (or appetizers) widely available throughout France are *soupe à l'oignon*, a thick onion soup topped with toasted bread and cheese; *quenelles de brochet*, pike-flavored dumplings served with a lobster sauce; *cuisses de grenouille*, frog's legs usually fried; and escargots, snails baked in the oven, usually with a garlic, parsley, and butter sauce. The national main course dishes include coq au vin, chicken cooked in a red wine sauce; *boeuf bourguignon*, a red wine beef stew; *navarin d'agneau*, another stew, this time made with lamb, white wine, and vegetables; *confit de canard*, duck cooked in its own fat; and *magret de canard*, duck breast.

The day starts with breakfast (*le petit déjeuner*), usually consisting of bread with butter and jelly or jam eaten with coffee or tea, traditionally served in bowls, not cups. *Le déjeuner* (lunch) is, by tradition, the biggest meal of the day. Most workplaces give their employees two hours for lunch; however, given workplace demands, dinner (*le diner*) has started to take over as the main meal of the day, when families often gather for conversation and relaxation. Meals are always accompanied by bread and water and often with wine.

Confit de canard, or duck leg, with white beans and watercress.

People line up at a French bakery.

The French eat less these days. In the not so distant past, and still available in some restaurants, a meal would consist of a starter, then a fish course, followed by the meat course, and then a cheese and a dessert course. A glass of calvados (an apple-based liquor) or a sorbet made from calvados was traditionally served.

French towns have a number of speciality food shops. The baker—quite often situated near the church!—sells bread (of course) but also pastries, cakes, quiches, and sometimes sandwiches. The butcher shop (*boucherie*) sells meat as well as rillettes—a kind of coarse pâté—along with sausages and the like. A delicatessen provides a range of salads, cold cuts, and cheeses. Le *poissonier* (fishmonger) sells fish from France's two coasts—the Atlantic and the Mediterranean—as well as seafood and shellfish. Of course supermarkets supply all of these, as well as fish from beyond France's shores, as expanding trade opens the country up to more foreign products.

A DIETARY MAINSTAY

Bread is an absolute staple in France, and so the baker is an important figure. There are usually two bakings a day, one starting very early in the morning, so there is bread for breakfast, and then another in the afternoon. The baker usually snatches some sleep around lunchtime.

A market takes place one or two days a week, depending on the size of a town. All sorts of produce, quite often sold by the growers or producers themselves, are available in their own stalls. Depending on the season, you can find stalls that sell just one thing, such as oysters, mushrooms, snails, and the like. The market is an important part of French life: it is a place to meet your friends and pass the time of day over a coffee or a glass of wine in the local café.

As in most countries, a vast range of restaurants exists in France, including small cafés and bistros up to high-end gastronomic establishments. Waiters take their jobs seriously, with schools of restaurant service giving diplomas. It is not usual to tip at a restaurant—only if you have greatly appreciated the service—as waiters' salaries reflect their training and professional status.

Except in the northwest, one can drive throughout France and see acres of vines, all neatly planted in rows. France has been making wine since 600 BC when Greek colonists settled in present-day Marseille. The Romans encouraged the growing of vines in other areas that would become the renowned wine regions of Burgundy, Bordeaux, Champagne, Alsace, the Loire Valley, Languedoc, and the Rhone. Before the French Revolution in 1789, a great deal of wine-producing land was owned by the Church. The priests and monks who tended the vineyards started to understand the terroir—the specific characteristics, such as soil and climate, of each area. In Beaujolais in eastern France, for example, wines grown on one side of a hill can taste completely different from those on the other side, even using the same *cépage* or grape variety.

Varieties of sausages in a French market.

A market display of French olives.

Cheese is usually served after the main course in a traditional French meal.

WHAT'S IN A LABEL?

The *appellation d'origine contrôllée* (AOC) is a certification given by the state to indicate the precise origin of a cheese or wine. The first was given to Roquefort in 1411 where it was regulated by a parliamentary decree. Other countries, such as Italy, have similar regulations, but no others are quite as strict as the French system.

The bubbly white wine known as champagne is one of France's best-known exports, and its origins are quite amusing. Because of the northerly climate of the region, the wines produced were a pale pinkish color with a high acidity and low sugar content. The growers, envious of neighboring Burgundy, wanted to make wine of equal quality. The cold temperatures would stop the fermentation, a process critical to winemaking, and the wine makers prematurely bottled the wine. However, the warmer spring weather would awaken the yeast still in the wine and the fermentation would start again. The wine makers were appalled, but the English grew to love this sparkling wine, finding favor among royalty and the wealthy, and so the reputation of champagne grew.

French cheeses are also quite varied, and nearly all regions have their own speciality. One of the most famous is camembert, a soft, creamy cheese with a white edible rind, coming from Normandy. Another is the blue cheese Roquefort, made in a small village in the south of France. Cheese can be made with milk from cows, sheep, or goats. Each has its distinctive flavor.

TEXT-DEPENDENT QUESTIONS

1. In your own words, define *terroir* and explain how it affects winemaking in France.

2. Describe two of the regional or national dishes of France that sound particularly appetizing or intriguing to you.

RESEARCH PROJECTS

1. Find a map of France online or in a book and create your own rough map, outlining and labelling the wine and food regions discussed in this chapter.

2. Use the Internet to research the process of winemaking or cheesemaking and write a two-three paragraph description of it.

Crêpes suzette, a classic French dessert.

Teacher and children on a field trip at the Louvre in Paris.

WORDS TO UNDERSTAND

consortium: an association or group made up of several companies.

distillation: purifying a liquid through heating and cooling.

maceration: softening something, especially with reference to food, by soaking in a liquid.

pneumatic: containing air or gas under pressure.

CHAPTER 4

School, Work, and Industry

Children are obliged to start school at the age of six but most start at three, when they attend an *école maternelle*, or kindergarten. While they participate in creative and artistic activities, these are not just playschools: students are taught reading, writing, numbers, and even occasionally a foreign language. At the age of six, children go to *école primaire* or *élémentaire*—primary or grade school. Similar to other countries, the pupils are taught math, the French language, geography and history, the arts, and a foreign language, usually English. From eleven to fifteen, children go to *collège*, or middle school. Here science, art and music, physical education, and civics are added to their studies.

Exterior of the Lycée Louis-le-Grand, on the Rue Saint-Jacques in Paris.

At the end of *collège* pupils take an examination known as the brevet and then either end their education (if they are at least sixteen) or continue to the *lycée*. In practice, over 90 percent choose to continue. The main function of the *lycée*, or high school, is to prepare the pupils for the *baccalauréat* (bac) exam. Subjects covered are the same as at the middle school but with the addition of philosophy in the final year.

Those choosing to continue their education can go on to university or, if they are exceptionally bright, to a *grande école*. There are eighty-one public universities in France plus twenty-three private ones, of which seven are Catholic and three Protestant. French public universities are legally obliged to accept all candidates from their region who hold a *baccalauréat*.

ELITE UNIVERSITIES IN FRANCE

The *grandes écoles* are elite schools outside the public university system. They will admit only those who have achieved a high standard in tough written and oral examinations, and many candidates spend two years of dedicated preparatory classes just to enter them. Most of France's high-ranking civil servants, politicians, and executives will have gone to a *grande école*.

Despite its current high unemployment rate (10 percent in 2014), work life in France helps define the country's cultural identity. Artisan craftwork, time-honored in France, employs more than 3 million, more than any other type of occupation. Often thought of as only working in stone, glass, metalwork, or wood, the category includes workers in more recent occupations such as graphic design and web development. Most artisans are self-employed.

About one-fifth of the workforce is in manufacturing, while over three-quarters are in the service industries. Agriculture is a key sector in the national economy, given the importance of food in French society, despite the fact that a decreasing share—only 2.5 percent—of the French are employed in it. And even though the workforce has been reduced by a factor of six since the 1950s, production volumes have tripled, growth made possible by mechanization, crop fertilization, and plant and animal selection. A large number of farmers have no employees: they work the land themselves.

Dating from the Middle Ages, an organization called Les Compagnons du Tour de France allows a young person to learn a trade while learning about themselves and experiencing community life. The name Tour de France has nothing to do with the cycle race, however! It refers to the fact that every six months the members are obliged to change work locations. They are capable of outstanding workmanship by the end of their nine years as a *compagnon*.

With 30 percent of the global market, France's perfume industry ranks at the top of the world. Although the big names in the perfume industry—including Chanel and Dior—are based in Paris, a little town in the

A village festival in Bouzeran, Burgundy, includes this blacksmith's demonstration.

south called Grasse has a rich history of perfume making. Its mild Mediterranean climate particularly suits the growing of flowers such as jasmine, lavender, roses, mimosa, and myrtle. With a population of just 44,000 inhabitants, 3,500 are employed by some sixty different companies. The methods of extracting the fragrances from flowers are by **distillation** or **maceration**—that is, soaking the petals in a liquid that absorbs the aromas. These concentrates, known as essential oils, are then blended to make the perfume.

A LA MODE!

French fashion houses are as famous as its perfumes—with Yves Saint Laurent and Pierre Cardin, as well as Dior and Chanel among others, among the top. But more avant-garde designers—such Isabel Marant and the Elisha Brothers—are also rocking the fashion world.

The world's leading tire manufacturer, Michelin, was founded and has its headquarters in Clermont Ferrand in southern central France. Since its founding in 1889 it has made a number of innovations. The first—in its first year—was the removable bicycle tire: previous **pneumatic** bicycle tires had to be glued to the wheel rims. In 1934 they introduced a tire that, if punctured, would run

The Fragonard perfumery is one of the older factories in Grasse, the world capital of perfumes. Pictured here in 2013 are shoppers inside the factory store.

The high-speed train, or TGV, between Paris and the eastern city of Strasbourg.

on a special foam lining, today known as the run-flat tire. In 1946 Michelin brought out the first radial tire, and the company now make tires for bicycles, cars, trucks, airplanes, and even tires for railways.

France has had a long-standing reputation in pursuing science and technology. For instance, radioactivity was discovered by a Frenchman, Henri Becquerel, and the foundations of Einstein's special relativity were laid down by mathematician and physicist Henri Poincaré. France tested its first atomic bomb in 1960 and its first hydrogen bomb in 1968 and now is number one in the world in terms of nuclear-generated electricity, with 75 percent produced in nuclear power stations. France launched its own space satellite in 1965, third after the former USSR and the United States.

In communications, France developed the Minitel in 1978—thought of as the world's most successful precursor to the Internet. Accessible using the normal telephone network, users could make train reservations, online purchases, search the telephone directory, check stock prices, and even have a mailbox and chat—all this before the World Wide Web came into existence!

France's rail network is extensive, reliable—and fast! Developed in the 1970s, the TGV (Train à Grande Vitesse, or high-speed train), with Paris as its hub, has a network linking many cities across the nation. In 2007 a TGV set the record for the fastest wheeled train, attaining a speed of 357 miles/hour (575 km/hour). Beginning construction in 1988 and opening in 1994, the Channel Tunnel, an Anglo-French project, links France with Great Britain. Carrying both the high-speed Eurostar passenger trains and the freight- and car-carrying Le Shuttle, it has carried over 20 million passengers and 21 million tons (19 million metric tonnes) of freight have since 1994.

The country's interest in air travel began long ago, with the invention of the hot air balloon by the Montgolfier brothers in 1783. The first passengers were a sheep, a rooster, and a duck! In 1909, Louis Blériot became the first man to cross the English Channel in a heavier-than-air aircraft as well as being the first to make a powered monoplane.

FLIGHTS OF FANCY

In 1894, Octave Chanute, born in France but living in the United States, published a book collecting all the technical data he could find on aviation. The Wright brothers used this reference as a basis for many of their experiments.

Today, Airbus, the biggest rival to U.S.-based Boeing, started as a **consortium** of aerospace manufacturers from four countries—France, Germany, Spain, and the United Kingdom. With headquarters in Toulouse in southern France and with employees numbering 63,000 at sixteen sites in the four countries, the company is an important employer in France. It made the Airbus 320, with the first commercially viable fly-by-wire (electronics-based) flight controls and currently

also makes the world's largest airliner, the Airbus 380.

Regarded by many as an engineering wonder and an aviation icon, the Condorde, produced jointly with Great Britain, was one of only two supersonic commercial passenger airliners, the other being the Russian Tupolev Tu-144. Traveling at twice the speed of sound, it could fly from Paris to New York in around three and a half hours—half the time taken by normal subsonic airliners. For financial reasons, the aircraft was retired in 2003.

A 1786 description of the Montgolfier Brothers' historic 1783 balloon flight.

TEXT-DEPENDENT QUESTIONS

1. What sector employs the most people in France? In what type of occupation do most French people earn a living?
2. Name the town in France important in the perfume industry and describe what makes it important.

RESEARCH PROJECTS

1. In a brief essay, describe the university system in France and compare it to the United States.
2. Select a famous French perfume, fashion, or transport company and write a brief history of it.

The newest in Air France's fleet, a double-decker Airbus 380, made in France.

Fête de la Musique, an annual music event, shown here in Paris.

WORDS TO UNDERSTAND

intrinsic: belonging naturally, or essential to something.

prestigious: inspiring admiration.

CHAPTER 5

Arts and Entertainment

The French use their leisure time in all sorts of ways—from sports to art, music, and cinema, activities to suit all sorts of tastes and interests. All avenues of entertainment are embraced with enthusiasm, good humor, and passion—the classic French "joie de vivre," or joy in living!

Intrinsic to French culture, participation in sports is high. The most popular is soccer, or football as it is called in many countries, with most towns, even small ones, having teams—some fielding both men and women's teams. Of course, the main teams are followed on television and in the newspapers as well. France hosted the FIFA World Cup in 1998, which it won. It was runner-up in 2006. The day after it won, *L'Équipe*, a daily newspaper focused on sports, sold 1,645,907 copies!

Ranking the second most popular sport is tennis. Every year, in the spring, the world's best international clay-court players converge on Roland Garros, or the French Open, in one of the most well-known tournaments in the tennis year. Named after a World War One fighter pilot who attended the tennis center in the 1920s, it has a distinctive red playing surface.

BALLET IS BORN!

While it originated in Italian Renaissance courts, ballet was developed in France. In fact most of the terminology comes from French with words and phrases such as *à la seconde, chassé, derrière, glissard, plié,* and *tutu.*

It is impossible to speak of popular French sports without mentioning cycling. All over France, usually at weekends, groups of cyclists in their brightly-colored-sponsored vests can be seen pedalling the challenging terrain of the French countryside. Of course the enthusiasm is rekindled each July as the world focuses its attention on the Tour de France. Now taking in other countries—

The peloton, or main pack of riders, climbing to the Col de Pailhères in the Pyrenees during the Tour de France on July 6, 2013.

Auguste and Louis Lumière, considered the inventors of cinema.

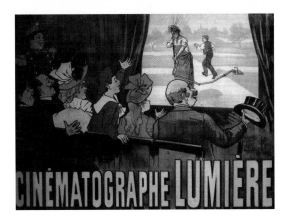

The poster advertising the Lumière brothers cinematograph, showing the comedy *L'Arroseur Arrosé*.

the 2014 race started in Great Britain and included a short stint in Belgium—the route is changed annually. It covers some very difficult terrain—notably in the Pyrenees in southwestern France and in the Alps and Vosges in the eastern part of the country—which, especially in wet weather, can be quite treacherous.

As you drive through French towns you will see areas of hard dirt or gravel in many public parks. These playing areas are for the game *pétanque*, or *boules*, where the goal is to throw heavy metal balls as close as possible to a small wooden ball called a *cochonnet* (literally piglet!), or jack, while standing behind a semicircle chalked or scraped in the fine gravel. Players can "bomb" the balls of their opponents to shift them further away from the jack.

Many forms of entertainment other than sport spark the French imagination, especially film. The French film industry has the third biggest market in the world with over 200 million tickets sold every year. In 2001, a comedy, *Amélie*, became the highest grossing French language film ever released in the United States. The Cannes International Film Festival, held annually in the spring, is one of the most **prestigious** and publicized festivals of its type, with producers, directors, and stars arriving from all over the world.

CINEMA OF LIGHT

The country is considered the birthplace of cinema: the brothers Lumière (coincidentally the French for "light") patented the cinematograph in 1895. It was a device that could be used as a moving picture camera as well as a projector.

Theme parks enliven towns and regions across the country. Near Poitiers in central France, Futuroscope, based on cinema, multimedia, and audio-visual techniques, has several 3-D and 4-D cinemas and five IMAX cinemas, including one that is "flying-carpet" style featuring a second screen on the floor. Other theme parks include Vulcania, located amongst a chain of extinct volcanoes in the central part of the country, which tells the story of how volcanoes are created; a visitor can experience what it feels like during an earthquake. Parc Asterix, located just a short distance north of Paris, is based on the comic books featuring Astérix and Obélix and has many rides and roller-coasters as well as different worlds to explore—Gaul and the famous Gaul village, the Roman Empire, ancient Greece, and the Vikings. Located just west of Paris is *France Miniature*, which has a map of France covering 5 hectares (nearly 12.5 acres), with 116 replicas of the most beautiful monuments and 150 model landscapes reproduced at one-thirtieth scale. You can visit the whole of France in just one day!

Most large towns and cities have museums or art galleries. Of course, the most well known are those in Paris, with the Louvre, the Centre Georges Pompidou, and the Musée d'Orsay, among others. The world's most visited painting, *La Gioconda*—the Mona Lisa—can be found in the Louvre, with about 6 million people a year coming to see it.

Specialized museums can be found across the country: there is a corkscrew museum near Marseille in the south; the world's largest collection of armored fighting vehicles in the Tank Museum at Saumur, in central France; a wallpaper museum in Alsace, in northeastern France; and even a museum of wild salmon, the *Odyssaum*, in Brittany, in the northwest.

A TRAIN STATION, A HOME FOR ART

The Musée d'Orsay in Paris—an art gallery housing the largest collection of Impressionist and Post-Impressionist paintings in the world—was once a railway station. Constructed in time for the 1900 Exposition Universelle, its short platform soon became unsuitable for the longer, mainline trains. It became a listed building in 1978 and opened as a gallery in 1986.

Music—in many forms—has been important throughout France's history. The romantic composers of the late nineteenth and early twentieth centuries—Berlioz,

Musée d'Orsay in Paris, a museum dedicated to Impressionist and Post-Impressionist art built from a former train station.

Bizet, Fauré, Ravel, and Debussy, to name just a few—have contributed to classical music output, and Erik Satie was another significant composer from the late nineteenth century. In 1900 Paris saw a new style of waltz emerge called the *valse musette*, typically played on the accordion, which is still very popular in France.

Cabaret music also began in the late 1800s and lasted until the 1930s, with the genre creating international stars such as Édith Piaf, Maurice Chevalier, and Charles Trenet. The 1950s and 1960s saw the likes of Mireille Mathieu, Juliette Greco, George Brassens, Jacques Brel, Sheila, and Françoise Hardy.

A type of theatrical entertainment also known as "cabaret," featuring music, dance, and comedy, started in Montmartre, a neighborhood in Paris surrounding the Catholic church of Sacre Coeur. The first to open was Le Chat Noir (The Black Cat) in 1881. Other famous venues are Le Moulin Rouge with its large red windmill (*moulin*) on the roof, the Folies Bergère, and Le Lido. Often the spectacle includes the cancan, an energetic and suggestive dance performed by female dancers wearing long skirts, petticoats, and black stockings, using high kicking and the lifting of their skirts. The African-American singer and dancer Josephine Baker was a main proponent of cabaret.

Jazz has long been appreciated in France, becoming important in the 1920s. Guitarist Django Reinhardt and violinist Stéphane Grappelli formed the

Quintette du Hot Club de France in 1934, and it played to dedicated fans until 1948. A jazz club in the Latin Quarter of Paris, Le Caveau de la Huchette, created in 1946 and still going today, is an important venue for both French and American jazz musicians, with greats such as Lionel Hampton, Count Basie, and Art Blakey having worked there. Today there are jazz festivals held all over France.

In 1981 the first annual Fête de la Musique, a massive celebration of music held on June 21st, the longest day of the year, began and is now celebrated all over the world. In France almost every town has several mostly amateur bands playing many different genres of music. Indeed, music is an important part of French cultural heritage.

Festivals draw many communities together throughout France. The national holiday, July 14th, celebrates the storming of the Bastille in 1789, an event that started the French Revolution. Festivities take place all over the country, with people wearing red, white, and blue to match the tricolor flag and firework displays in the evening. On January 6, Christian families celebrate the Epiphany or Twelfth Night with a large flat pastry cake, traditionally filled with frangipane (almond paste).

Throughout the year, towns and villages hold their own fête day as well, often with special themes relating to the regions' agricultural or gastronomic specialties, including Fête du Champignons (a mushroom festival) or a Fête des Omelettes, during which a giant omelette containing 15,000 eggs is cooked

in a huge pan. In Menton in the south of France, a Fête du Citron (lemon festival) is held every spring, attracting over 250,000 visitors and using 160 tons (145 metric tonnes) of citrus fruit.

Lemon Festival (Fête du Citron) on the French Riviera in the south of France.

TEXT-DEPENDENT QUESTIONS

1. What is *pétanque*, where is it played, and what is the object of the game?

2. Describe Fête de la Musique, including when was it founded, when it takes place, and what is involved.

RESEARCH PROJECTS

1. Select one painting that interests you from one of the major French museums in Paris. Describe what it looks like and what it makes you think of and feel in two to three brief paragraphs.

2. Research one of the popular sports in France and compare it to a popular U.S. sport. Compare attendance and earnings in a table and write a brief summary of your findings.

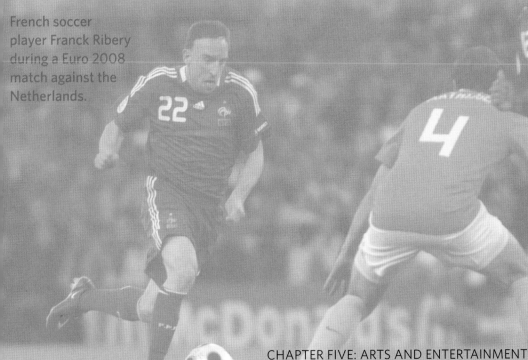

French soccer player Franck Ribery during a Euro 2008 match against the Netherlands.

Mont St. Michel in Normandy, on the north coast of France.

WORDS TO UNDERSTAND

barbican: a tower on the defending walls of a town, usually with a gate or bridge.

guillotine: an old, simple machine used for executions by beheadin

obelisk: a tall pillar-like monument with four sides.

raze: to knock to the ground.

viaduct: a raised road used to move people, cars, trains, and the like from one place to another.

CHAPTER 6

Cities, Towns, and the Countryside

The landscape of France blends its rich culture and human industry in easy harmony with its natural beauty. From the sophistication of its forty-two *grand villes*, or major cities, to the countryside dotted with breathtaking natural beauty and pretty villages, the country embraces both the ancient and modern at the same time.

The grandest of France's *grand villes* is Paris, its capital. It wasn't until the mid-nineteenth century that the city took on much of its current look. Emperor Napoleon III employed Baron Haussmann to replace the maze of winding, narrow streets dating back to the Middle Ages that made up the city center. Over 2,000 buildings were **razed**, and some forty streets were leveled and replaced by 125 miles (200 kilometres) of wide boulevards lined with generous sidewalks and street lighting—and sewers as well.

The city is divided into twenty arrondissements (administrative districts) arranged in a clockwise spiral starting from the middle, with the first on the Right Bank, or north side, of the River Seine, a major geographic and cultural artery of the city. It is not the only city in France to be subdivided like this: Lyon and Marseille are similar.

The First Arrondissement is home to the Louvre, the city's most important museum. From the Louvre a long axis begins with an unobstructed view through the Tuileries Gardens, past the Luxor **Obelisk**, imported from the Egyptian Temple of Luxor, in the Place de la Concorde. This is the largest public square in Paris and was the site of the executions by **guillotine** during the French Revolution. The Avenue des Champs-Elysées continues the axis and rises up to the Place Charles de Gaulle, historically known as Place de l'Étoile (French for "star"), which is the meeting point of twelve straight avenues with the Arc de Triomphe in its center.

A WORLD-CLASS AVENUE
The Champs-Élysées is perhaps Paris's most famous avenue, measuring 1.2 miles (1.9 kilometers) long and 76 yards (69.5 meters) wide. It is flanked by art museums, luxury shops, theatres, and cafés, as well as the Élysée Palace, which is the home of the French president.

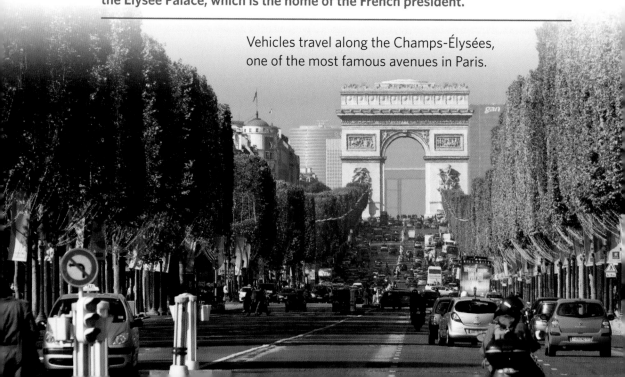

Vehicles travel along the Champs-Élysées, one of the most famous avenues in Paris.

During Lyon's annual Festival of Lights, the city's main church is brightly lit up, including the words "Merci Marie," showing gratitude to the Virgin Mary for saving the city from the plague.

Of course, Paris is famous for other buildings as well, such as the twelfth-century cathedral Notre Dame de Paris, the Eiffel Tower, and Les Invalides (the burial place of Napoleon I and his son Napoleon II, as well as many of France's great military heroes). The Basilica du Sacré-Coeur, a church built on the capital's highest point, in the district of Montmartre, is renowned for once being the home of many famous artists. Vincent van Gogh, Pablo Picasso, Claude Monet, Piet Mondrian, Amedeo Modigliani, and Salvador Dali all had studios there at one time.

The second largest metropolitan area of France, Lyon, is in the east-central part of the country at the confluence of the rivers Rhône and Saône. The former rises in Switzerland while the latter's source is in the northeast of France. Where they converge in Lyon, each has a very distinctive color: the Rhône is icy blue, and the Saône is a dark green color. For tens of meters after they meet, the river remains divided in two, colorwise, before eventually blending together. Lyon boasts well over 1,000 restaurants and eateries, bringing together flavors of the north—with its reliance on cream and butter—and the south—with its focus on olive oil and fresh produce.

THE CAPITAL OF LIGHTS

Lyon is known as the Capital of Lights due to the legend that the Virgin Mary saved the populace from the plague, and the city built a statue to thank her. On the day it was erected, the whole city was lit by candles. A four-day festival of lights every year in December, which attracts over 4 million tourists, celebrates the city's homage to Mary.

Marseille, in the southeast of the country, is the third largest metropolitan area in France. The country's only major port on the Mediterranean, the city became a center for maritime trade that flourished even more with the building of Egypt's Suez Canal in 1869. Being a port, Marseille is a cosmopolitan city, with immigrants coming from Greece and Italy at the end of the nineteenth century and other nationalities in the twentieth century, including North African Arabs and Berbers in the 1960s. Today over a third of the population can trace their ancestors back to Italy.

Smaller towns of France have a distinctly regional appearance, with building materials reflecting their geographical surroundings. In the northeast, towns such as Colmar in Alsace have half-timbered houses built along the banks of the River Lauch. In the Loire Valley, in central France, towns such as Saumur almost glow in the sunlight due to the creamy-yellow-colored Tuffeau stone used in the construction of many of the buildings. Tuffeau, a rock particular to the Loire Valley, is formed from increasing layers of sediment, comprising fossilized organisms and sand particles. Huge amounts have been quarried over the ages to be used in the construction of buildings ranging in size from small houses to huge châteaus. In Brittany, in the coastal northwest, many granite buildings can be found—either in gray or in a pinkish color for those on the Côte de Granit Rose, or Pink Granite Coast.

The medieval fortress and walled city of Carcassonne in southwest France. Founded by the Visigoths in the fifth century, it was restored in 1853 and is now a UNESCO World Heritage Site.

A WALLED FORTIFICATION

Carcassonne, a town in the south near the Pyrenees, was once completely enclosed within two sets of fortified walls and turrets. Of great strategic importance since even before they arrived, Romans began building the fortifications. Added to over the years, it now consists of a concentric design with fifty-three towers and **barbicans.**

A familiar sight in many towns is the restaurant, bar, or café with tables outside on the sidewalk. A rendezvous point for gossip and lively conversation, you can extend your meal over coffee and watch the world go by—the original social network! The buildings are from all eras, but the most spectacular come from the Belle Époque (Beautiful Era) of the late nineteenth century; the Art Nouveau period of the early twentieth; and the Art Deco period of the 1920s and 1930s. Some have retained the original details and can be extravagant, even exuberant—all mirrors and interesting light fittings—and feasts for the eyes as well as the stomach!

Due to France's diverse geography and geology, small towns and villages can vary enormously in appearance. The flat plains of the west and north can feature mile upon mile of fields of cereal crops, such as wheat and barley, punctuated by the telltale spires of the local village churches. Along the banks of the River Dordogne, in central France, can be found small towns and villages crammed beneath rocky cliffs at the very edges of the water, or at the tops of the hills themselves— perched on the rocks in places seemingly impossible to build upon.

Argentat, in south-central France, on the Dordogne River at sunrise on a still morning.

The Millau Viaduct, spanning the Tarn Valley in the Aveyron region of France.

A TOWERING BUT ELEGANT GIANT

The Millau Viaduct, remarkable in its elegance and simplicity, can be seen from miles around. One mast of the bridge rises some 1,125 feet (343 meters) above the valley below, making the viaduct the tallest bridge in the world.

Rivers indeed shape the landscape throughout the country, and many villages and small towns are sited along river courses, once crucial for transportation and some still important for small-scale power generation. The gorges carved by these rivers, most in the south—such as, from west to east, the Galamus, the Tarn, the Ardèche, and the Verdon—form steep walls and high precipices, offering dramatic views from either the high ridges or river bottoms.

Spectacular crossings over these river beds thrill those touring the country-side. For example, the ancient Roman aqueduct known as Pont du Gard—a UNESCO World Heritage site—spans the river Gard. And in the Millau **Viaduct**, a modern example that spans the river Tarn on a highway connecting Paris with the south, one can see the blending of culture, the built environment, and natural landscape that makes France such a compelling and memorable destination.

TEXT-DEPENDENT QUESTIONS

1. What is an arrondissement?
2. Describe the importance of rivers in France, citing examples both in cities and in the countryside.

RESEARCH PROJECTS

1. Write a report on one of the three most populous cities in France, with sections devoted to location and physical layout, to people and culture, and to economic life.
2. Gather photos of two to three small towns in one region or department of France along with photos of small towns in your area. In small groups, discuss your findings.

Blossoming lavender fields in Provence, in the southeast of France.

FURTHER RESEARCH

Online

Visit the Central Intelligence Agency's World Factbook to view statistics, a brief history, and various maps of France: https://www.cia.gov/library/publications/the-world-fact-book/geos/fr.html.

Learn more about tourism in France by visiting http://int.rendezvousenfrance.com.

Visit http://www.frenchculture.org to learn more about the many aspects of culture in France, including books, music, performing arts, and film.

Books

Abramson, Julia L. *Food Culture in France.* Westport, CT: Greenwood, 2006. A comprehensive look at food and its cultural context throughout the country.

Asselin, Giles, and Ruth Mastron. *Au Contraire: Figuring Out the French.* 2nd ed. Boston: Intercultural Press, 2010. This book offers an engaging study of cultural practices in France, with an emphasis on both cultural differences and similarities.

Jones, Colin. *The Cambridge Illustrated History of France.* New York: Cambridge University Press, 1999. An engaging and visually rich presentation of French history.

NOTE TO EDUCATORS: This book contains both imperial and metric measurements as well as references to global practices and trends in an effort to encourage the student to gain a worldly perspective. We, as publishers, feel it's our role to give young adults the tools they need to thrive in a global society.

SERIES GLOSSARY

ancestral: relating to ancestors, or relatives who have lived in the past.

archaeologist: a scientist that investigates past societies by digging in the earth to examine their remains.

artisanal: describing something produced on a small scale, usually handmade by skilled craftspeople.

colony: a settlement in another country or place that is controlled by a "home" country.

commonwealth: an association of sovereign nations unified by common cultural, political, and economic interests and traits.

communism: a social and economic philosophy characterized by a classless society and the absence of private property.

continent: any of the seven large land masses that constitute most of the dry land on the surface of the earth.

cosmopolitan: worldly; showing the influence of many cultures.

culinary: relating to the kitchen, cookery, and style of eating.

cultivated: planted and harvested for food, as opposed to the growth of plants in the wild.

currency: a system of money.

demographics: the study of population trends.

denomination: a religious grouping within a faith that has its own organization.

dynasty: a ruling family that extends across generations, usually in an autocratic form of government, such as a monarchy.

ecosystems: environments where interdependent organisms live.

endemic: native, or not introduced, to a particular region, and not naturally found in other areas.

exile: absence from one's country or home, usually enforced by a government for political or religious reasons.

feudal: a system of economic, political, or social organization in which poor landholders are subservient to wealthy landlords; used mostly in relation to the Middle Ages.

globalization: the processes relating to increasing international exchange that have resulted in faster, easier connections across the world.

gross national product: the measure of all the products and services a country produces in a year.

heritage: tradition and history.

homogenization: the process of blending elements together, sometimes resulting in a less interesting mixture.

iconic: relating to something that has become an emblem or symbol.

idiom: the language particular to a community or class; usually refers to regular, "everyday" speech.

immigrants: people who move to and settle in a new country.

indigenous: originating in and naturally from a particular region or country.

industrialization: the process by which a country changes from a farming society to one that is based on industry and manufacturing.

SERIES GLOSSARY

integration: the process of opening up a place, community, or organization to all types of people.

kinship: web of social relationships that have a common origin derived from ancestors and family.

literacy rate: the percentage of people who can read and write.

matriarchal: of or relating to female leadership within a particular group or system.

migrant: a person who moves from one place to another, usually for reasons of employment or economic improvement.

militarized: warlike or military in character and thought.

missionary: one who goes on a journey to spread a religion.

monopoly: a situation where one company or state controls the market for an industry or product.

natural resources: naturally occurring materials, such as oil, coal, and gold, that can be used by people.

nomadic: describing a way of life in which people move, usually seasonally, from place to place in search of food, water, and pastureland.

nomadic: relating to people who have no fixed residence and move from place to place.

parliament: a body of government responsible for enacting laws.

patriarchal: of or relating to male leadership within a particular group or system.

patrilineal: relating to the relationship based on the father or the descendants through the male line.

polygamy: the practice of having more than one spouse.

provincial: belonging to a province or region outside of the main cities of a country.

racism: prejudice or animosity against people belonging to other races.

ritualize: to mark or perform with specific behaviors or observances.

sector: part or aspect of something, especially of a country's or region's economy.

secular: relating to worldly concerns; not religious.

societal: relating to the order, structure, or functioning of society or community.

socioeconomic: relating to social and economic factors, such as education and income, often used when discussing how classes, or levels of society, are formed.

statecraft: the ideas about and methods of running a government.

traditional: relating to something that is based on old historical ways of doing things.

urban sprawl: the uncontrolled expansion of urban areas away from the center of the city into remote, outlying areas.

urbanization: the increasing movement of people from rural areas to cities, usually in search of economic improvement, and the conditions resulting this migration.

INDEX

Italicized page numbers refer to illustrations.

A

Africa 14, 52
agriculture 10, 26, 29, *29*, 35
Airbus company 38, *39*
Amélie (2001) 43
apple tart *(tarte tatin)* 26
architecture *19*, 44, *45*, 49–53
Arroseur Arrosé, L' (1895) *43*
art and design 9, *11*, 13, *13*, 35, 44, 47, 51
artisanal craftwork 35, *35*
Austria 12, 13
aviation industry 38, *39*

B

Baker, Josephine 45
ballet 42
Basie, Count (William) 46
Basilica du Sacré-Coeur (Paris) 45, 51
Bastille Day 46
Battle of Waterloo 13
Becquerel, Henri 37
Belgium 13, 43
Berlioz, Hector 44
birth rate 23
Bizet, Georges 45
Blakey, Art 46
Blériot, Louis 38
Bonaparte, Napoleon (Napoleon I; emperor of
        France) 12–13
Bonaparte, Louis Napoleon (nephew of
        Napoleon I) 13
Bordeaux 19
Brassens, George 45
bread 28, *28*
Brel, Jacques 45
Britain 10–12, 14, 37, 38

C

cabaret 45
Caesar, Julius Gaius 10
Cannes International Film Festival 43
Carcassonne (Languedoc-Roussillon) *52*, 53
Catherine de Medici (queen of France) 11, *11*
Catholic Church 11, 29, 34
cave paintings 9
Celts 10
Centre Georges Pompidou
        (museum in Paris) 44
champagne 30
Champs-Elysées, Avenue des (Paris) 50, *50*
Chanel S.A. 35–36
Channel Tunnel 37
Chanute, Octave 38
Charles IV (king of France) 10
Charles X (king of France) 13
cheese and cheesemaking 14, 26, *30*, 30–31
Chevalier, Maurice 45
children 18, 23, *32*
Christian Dior S.A. 35–36
cinematograph 43
cities *19*, 36, *36*, 39, 49, 50–52, *51*, 55. *See
        also* Marseille; Paris
Civil Solidarity Pact (PACS) 17–18
class system 18–19, 23
Compagnons du Tour de France 35
constitution 12, 13
crêpes Suzette *31*
Crimean War (1854–1856) 13
cultural identity 7, 14
cycling *42*, 42–43

D

Dali, Salvador 51
dancing 42, 45
David, Jacques-Louis *13*

INDEX

D-Day (Normandy invasion, World War II) 14, *14*
Debussy, Claude 45
de Gaulle, Charles 14, *15*
divine right of kings 12
Dordogne River 53, *53*
Dubois, François *11*

E
Edict of Nantes (1598) 11
education *32*, 33–35, *34*
Eiffel Tower (Paris) 7, *8*, 13, 51
Eleanor of Aquitane (queen consort of France) 10
Elisha brothers 36
elite universities *(grandes écoles)* 34
Emperor Napoleon in His Study at the Tuileries (David) *13*
Équipe, L' (newspaper) 41
etiquette 21, 23
Exposition Universelle (1889) 13
Exposition Universelle (1900) 44

F
family benefits 18
family roles and traditions *16*, 17–20, *18*, 22, 22
farmers' markets 29, *29*
fashion industry 36, 39
Fauré, Gabriel 45
Fête de la Musique (music festival, Paris) *40*, 46, 47
feudal system 10, 15
film industry 43, *43*
First French Empire 12–13
food and culinary traditions 14, 25–31, *26*, *27*, *28*, *29*, *30*, *31*
Fragonard Parfumeur *36*
François I (king of France) 11
Franco-Prussian War (1870–1871) 13

Franks 10
French Open tennis tournament (Roland Garros) 42
French Revolution (1789–1799) 9, 12, 19, 46
French Riviera *20*, 46
friendship *21*, 21–23

G
games 43, 47
Garros, Roland 42
Gaul 10
geography 7, 26, 53–55
Germany 13, 38
Gioconda, La (Mona Lisa, da Vinci) 44
Grandmother's Day *22*
Grappelli, Stéphane 45–46
Grasse 36, *36*, 39
Greco, Juliette 45
Greece 29, 52
greetings *21*, 21–22

H
Hampton, Lionel 46
Hardy, Françoise 45
Haussmann, Baron (George-Eugène) 49
Henry II (king of England) 10
Henry II (king of France) 11
Henry IV (king of France) 11
holiday celebrations and traditions 19, 20, *20*, 46, *51*
Huguenots 11
Hundred Years' War 10

I
immigration 14, 52
industry 14, 35–39
Intangible Cultural Heritage (UNESCO) 25–26
Isabel Marant company 36
Italy 11, 13, 30, 52

INDEX

J
jazz 45–46
Joan of Arc 10–11

K
kissing 21

L
Labor strikes 14, 20
landscape 7, *48*, 49, 53–54, *55*
language 10, 22–23, 33
leisure activities 41, 43–46
Lemon Festival (French Riviera) 46
liberation of Paris (1944) 14, *15*
"Liberté, égalité, fraternité" motto
            (freedom, equality, fraternity) 12
literacy rate 23
Louis VII (king of the Franks) 10
Louis XIV (king of France) 12, *12*
Louis XVIII (king of France) 13
Louvre Museum (Paris) *6*, *32*, 44, 50
Lumière brothers 43, *43*
Lycée Louis-le-Grand (Paris) *34*
Lyon 50, 51, *51*

M
marriage traditions 17–18
Marseille *16*, 19, 26, 29, 44, 50, 52
Mathieu, Mireille 45
May 1968 unrest 14
mealtime traditions 19, 21–22, *24*, 30
Michelin company 36–37
Middle Ages 10, 15, 49
Millau Viaduct (Aveyron) 54, *54*
Minitel 37
Modigliani, Amedeo 51
Mona Lisa (*La Gioconda*, da Vinci) 44
Mondrian, Piet 51
Monet, Claude 51
Montgolfier brothers 38, *38*

Montmartre 45
Mont St. Michel (Normandy) 48
Musée d'Orsay (Paris) 44, *45*
music *40*, 44–46

N
Napoleon Bonaparte (Napoleon I;
            emperor of France) 12–13
Nazi Germany 14
Netherlands 12, 13
Nice *20*
Normandy, Duke of 10
Normandy invasion (World War II) 14
Normans 10
Notre Dame de Paris cathedral 51
nuclear power 37

P
Paris *6*, 14, *15*, 19, *19*, *40*, 44, *45*, 49–51
perfume industry 35–36, *36*, 39
Piaf, Édith 45
Picasso, Pablo 51
Pierre Cardin 36
Plantagenet, House of 10
Poincaré, Henri 37
Pont du Gard *10*, 15, 54
pope 10, 12–13
population growth and distribution 23
Protestantism 11, 34
Provence *55*
Prussia 12
Pyrenees mountains *42*, *43*, 53

R
railroads *37*, 37–39
Ravel, Maurice 45
Reduction of Working Time (RTT—Réduction
            du Temps de Travail) 20
regional cooking 26–27, 31
Reign of Terror 12

INDEX

Reinhardt, Django 45–46
religion 10–13, 34, 51, *51*
Renaissance 11
rivers 50–51, *53*, 53–54, 55
Roland Garros (French Open tennis
          tournament) 42
Roman Empire 10, *10*, 15, 53
Russia 13

S
St. Bartholomew's Day massacre 11, *11*
St. Joan of Arc 10–11
Sargent, Robert F. *14*
Satie, Erik 45
science and technology 37
Second French Empire 13
Second Opium War 13
Seine River 50
Sheila (Annie Chancel) 45
soccer 41
Spain 12, 13, 38
sports 41–43, 47
supersonic airliners 38

T
Tatin, Stéphanie 26
tennis 42
terroir 29, 31
TGV high-speed trains (Trains à Grande
          Vitesse) 37, *37*
theme parks 44
Third Republic 13
tire production 36–37
Tour de France cycling race *42*, 42–43
towns and villages *35*, 46, *46*, 52–55
transportation system *37*, 37–39, 54–55
Trenet, Charles 45

U
unemployment 14, 35
university system 34, 39

V
vacations 20, *20*
Valois, House of 10
van Gogh, Vincent 51
Versailles *12*
Vichy France government 14
village culture (France Profonde) 19
Vosges Mountains 43

W
Wars of Religion (1562–1598) 11
William the Conqueror (king of France) 10
wine and winemaking industry 27, 29–31
World Heritage site (UNESCO) *52*, 54
World War I 14–15
World War II *14*, 14–15
Wright brothers 38

Y
Yves Saint Laurent 36

PHOTO CREDITS

Page	Page Location	Archive/Photographer	Page	Page Location	Archive/Photographer
6	Full page	Dreamstime/Alicja Ludwikowska	30	Top	Dreamstime/Yulia Davidovich
8	Top	Dreamstime/Zuperpups	31	Bottom	Dreamstime/Maffboy
10	Top left	Wikimedia Commons/Viktor Vasnetosov	32	Top	Dreamstime/Billkret
			34	Top	Dreamstime/Pavel Losevsky
11	Top right	Wikimedia Commons/Viktor Vasnetosov	35	Top right	Wikimedia Commons
			35	Bottom	Dreamstime/Eagleflying
12	Top left	Dreamstime/Vvoevale	36	Top left	Dollar Photo Club/cityanimal
12	Top right	Wikimedia Commons/Johann Vedikind	36	Bottom	Dreamstime/Aleksandr Bryliaev
13	Top right	Wikimedia Commons/Fyodor Rokotov	37	Top	Wikimedia Commons/Bin im Garten
13	Bottom	Dollar Photo Club/tomalu	38	Bottom	Dreamstime/2bears
14	Top left	Wikimedia Commons/Ivan Vladimirov	39	Bottom	Dreamstime/Rogkoff
14	Bottom right	Dreamstime/Fotomy	40	Top	Dreamstime/Alenmax
15	Bottom	Dreamstime/Pikoli	42	Top	Wikimedia Commons/Dmitry Kryukov
17	Top	Dreamstime/Iakov Filimonov	43	Bottom right	Wikimedia Commons
18	Top	Dreamstime/Olgavolodina	44	Bottom left	Dreamstime/Ivan Varyukhin
19	Top right	Dreamstime/Iakov Filimonov	44	Bottom right	Dreamstime/Pavel Losevsky
19	Bottom left	Abcgallery.com/Henryk Siemiradzki	45	Top right	Wikimedia Commons
20	Bottom left	Dreamstime/Baibaz	46	Top left	Dreamstime/Afonskaya Irina
21	Top right	Dollar Photo Club/Ankor	46	Bottom left	Dreamstime/Iakov Filimonov
21	Bottom	Dreamstime/Photocell	47	Bottom	Dreamstime/Igor Dolgov
22	Top	Dreamstime/Igor Dolgov	48	Top	Dollar Photo Club/Mikhail Markovskiy
22	Middle right	Dollar Photo Club/olya_dn	50	Top left	Dollar Photo Club/Pavel Losevsky
23	Bottom	Dreamstime/Konstantin Pukhov	50	Top right	Dollar Photo Club/Nikolai Sorokin
25	Top	Dreamstime/Toxawww	51	Bottom right	Dollar Photo Club/Brian Kinney
26	Top left	Dreamstime/Ppy2010ha	52	Bottom left	Dollar Photo Club/lexan
26	Top right	Dreamstime/Olga Kriger	53	Top	Dreamstime/Artem Mishukov
27	Bottom	Dreamstime/Jjspring	54	Top	Dollar Photo Club/danr13
28	Top	Wikimedia Commons/	54	Bottom	Dreamstime/Sergge
28	Bottom right	Dreamstime/Dmitrv Bodyaev	55	Bottom	Dreamstime/Mathes
29	Bottom	Dreamstime/Natalia Pavlova			

COVER

Top	Gerald Reisner
Bottom left	Dreamstime/Ekaterina Pokrovsky
Bottom right	Gerald Reisner

ABOUT THE AUTHOR

Born and bred in the United Kingdom, **Richard Garratt** initially worked as a designer for the publishers Macmillan, David and Charles, and Oxford University Press before becoming a freelance designer and the design director for Curtis Garratt Limited—a small, independent design/editorial company specializing in the production of nonfiction books.

With the rise of computer-based production methods and the ease of file transferral, he seized the opportunity to live and work in France, where he specializes in providing high-quality content for a wide range of nonfiction publications, including illustrations and maps for encyclopedias and other reference works.

A publishing all-rounder, Richard has worked for many clients in the United States, the United Kingdom, France, and Japan.